Itty Bitty
Dress-Up Fashions™

Bridal Set

SKILL LEVEL

INTERMEDIATE

FINISHED SIZE
Fits 5-inch baby doll

MATERIALS
- Super fine (fingering) weight yarn:
  3½ oz/263 yds/100g white
- Size B/1/2.25mm crochet hook
  or size needed to obtain gauge
- Tapestry needle
- Sewing needle
- White sewing thread
- Snap
- ¼-inch-wide pink ribbon: 6 inches
- ¼-inch ribbon roses:
    13 white
    25 pink
- Tiny pearl beads:
    8 each pink and white
- 7 x 16-inch piece white tulle
- Stitch markers

1 SUPER FINE

GAUGE
7 sc = 1 inch; 8 sc rows = 1 inc

Row 4: Ch 1, sc in each st across, turn.

SKIRT
Row 5: Working in **back lps** (*see Stitch Guide*), ch 1, sc in first st, [ch 3, sc in next st] across, turn. *(37 ch sps)*

Row 6: Sl st in first ch sp, ch 1, sc in same ch sp, [ch 3, sc in next ch sp across, turn.

Row 7: Ch 1, sc in first st, ch 3, sc in first ch sp, [ch 3, sc in next ch sp] across, ch 3, sc in last st, turn.

Rnd 8: Now working in rnds, sl st in first ch sp, ch 1, sc in same ch sp, [ch 3, sc in next ch sp] around, ch 1, join with dc in beg sc, forming last ch sp.

Rnds 9–14: Ch 1, sc in last ch sp formed, [ch 3, sc in next ch sp] around, ch 1, join with dc in beg sc forming ch sp.

PATTERN NOTES
Join with slip stitch as indicated unless otherwise stated.

Chain-3 at beginning of row or round counts as first double crochet unless otherwise stated.

Do not apply small beads or buttons to doll clothing that is intended for play by children ages 3 or less.

INSTRUCTIONS
GOWN
Row 1: Beg at neckline, ch 25, 2 sc in 2nd ch from hook and in each ch across, turn. *(48 sc)*

Row 2 (RS): Ch 1, sc in each of first 8 sts, ch 5, sk next 10 sts *(armhole)*, sc in each of next 12 sts, ch 5, sk next 10 sts *(armhole)*, sc in each of last 8 sts, turn. *(10 chs, 28 sc)*

Row 3: Ch 1, sc in first st and in each st and ch across, turn. *(38 sc)*

FIRST SECTION
Row 1: Now working in rows, ch 1, sc in last ch sp formed, [ch 3, sc in next ch sp] 9 times, mark last ch sp worked in, leaving rem ch sps unworked, turn.

Row 2: Sl st in first ch sp, ch 1, sc in same ch sp, [ch 3, sc in next ch sp] across, turn.

Rows 3–9: Rep row 2. At end of last row, fasten off. *(1 lp at end of last row)*

2ND & 3RD SECTIONS
Row 1: Join *(see Pattern Notes)* in marked ch sp, ch 1, sc in same ch sp, [ch 3, sc in next ch sp] 9 times, mark last ch sp worked in, leaving rem ch sps unworked, turn.

Rows 2–9: Rep rows 2–9 of First Section.

4TH SECTION
Row 1: Join in marked ch sp, ch 1, sc in same ch sp, [ch 3, sc in next ch sp] 9 times, leaving rem ch sps unworked, turn.

Rows 2–9: Rep rows 2–9 of First Section, **do not fasten off** at end of last row.

EDGING

Rnd 1: Working around entire outer edge, ch 1, 3 sc in each ch sp and 2 sc in end of each row around with 3 sc in each ch sp on rnd 9, join in beg sc, **turn.** *(134 sc)*

Rnd 2: Ch 1, (sc, ch 6, sc) in first st, ch 6, [(sc, ch 6, sc) in next st, ch 6] around, join in beg sc. Fasten off.

UNDERSKIRT

Row 1: Working in rem lps on row 4 of Gown, join in first st, **ch 3** *(see Pattern Notes)*, dc in same st, 2 dc in each st across, turn. *(76 dc)*

Row 2: Ch 3, dc in same st, dc in next st, [2 dc in next st, dc in next st] across, turn. *(114 dc)*

Rnd 3: Now working in rnds, ch 3, dc in each st around, join in 3rd ch of beg ch-3.

Rnds 4 & 5: Ch 3, dc in each st around, join in 3rd ch of beg ch-3.

Rnd 6: Ch 3, dc in each of next 17 sts, 2 dc in next st, [dc in each of next 18 sts, 2 dc in next st] around, join in 3rd ch of beg ch-3. *(120 dc)*

Rnd 7: Ch 1, sc in each of first 16 sts, *working in **front lps** *(see Stitch Guide)*, [(sc, ch 6, sc) in next st, ch 6] 3 times, (sc, ch 6, sc) in next st**, working in both lps, sc in each of next 26 sts, rep from * around, ending last rep at **, working in both lps, sc in each of last 10 sts, join in beg sc.

Rnd 8: Ch 3, dc in each of next 15 sts, working in rem lps of rnd 6, dc in each of next 4 sts, [working in both lps, dc in each of next 26 sts, working in rem lps on rnd 6, dc in each of next 4 sts] 3 times, working in both lps, dc in each of last 10 sts, join in 3rd ch of beg ch-3.

Rnd 9: Ch 1, sc in each of first 14 sts, *working in front lps, [(sc, ch 6, sc) in next st, ch 6] 7 times, (sc, ch 6, sc) in next st**, working in both lps, sc in each of next 22 sts, rep from * around, ending last rep at **, working in both lps, sc in each of last 8 sts, join in beg sc.

Rnd 10: Ch 3, dc in each of next 13 sts, working in rem lps of sts on rnd 8, dc in each of next 8 sts, [working in both lps, dc in each of next 22 sts, working in rem lps on rnd 8, dc in each of next 8 sts] 3 times, working in both lps, dc in each of last 8 sts, join in 3rd ch of beg ch-3.

Rnd 11: Ch 1, sc in each of first 12 sts, *working in front lps, [(sc, ch 6, sc) in next st, ch 6] 11 times, (sc, ch 6, sc) in next st**, working in both lps, sc in each of next 18 sts, rep from * around, ending last rep at **, working in both lps, sc in each of last 6 sts, join in beg sc.

Rnd 12: Ch 3, dc in each of next 11 sts, working in rem lps of sts on rnd 10, dc in each of next 12 sts, [working in both lps, dc in each of next 18 sts, working in rem lps on rnd 10, dc in each of next 12 sts] 3 times, working in both lps, dc in each of last 6 sts, join in 3rd ch of beg ch-3.

Rnd 13: Ch 1, sc in each of first 10 sts, *working in front lps, [(sc, ch 6, sc) in next st, ch 6] 15 times, (sc, ch 6, sc) in next st**, working in both lps, sc in each of next 14 sts, rep from * around, ending last rep at **, working in both lps, sc in each of last 4 sts, join in beg sc.

Rnd 14: Ch 3, dc in each of next 9 sts, working in rem lps of sts on rnd 12, dc in each of next 16 sts, [working in both lps, dc in each of next 14 sts, working in rem lps on rnd 12, dc in each of next 16 sts] 3 times, working in both lps, dc in each of last 4 sts, join in 3rd ch of beg ch-3.

Rnd 15: Working in front lps, ch 1, (sc, ch 6, sc) in first st, ch 6, [(sc, ch 6, sc) in next st, ch 6] around, join in beg sc.

Rnd 16: Working in back lps of rnd 14, ch 1, (sc, ch 6, sc) in first st, ch 6, [(sc, ch 6, sc) in next st, ch 6] around, join in beg sc. Fasten off.

SLEEVES

Rnd 1: Working on opposite side of ch-5 of armholes, join in center ch, ch 1, sc in same ch, sc in each of next 2 chs, 2 sc in end of next row, sc in each of next 10 sts, 2 sc in end of next row, sc in each of last 2 chs, join in beg sc. *(19 sc)*

Rnd 2: Ch 1, sc in first st, [ch 3, sc in next st] around, ch 1, join with dc in beg sc, forming ch sp.

Rnd 3: Ch 1, sc in ch sp just formed, [ch 3, sc in next ch sp] around, ch 1, join with dc in beg sc.

Rnd 4: Rep rnd 3.

Rnd 5: Ch 1, sc in ch sp just formed, sc in each ch sp around, join in beg sc. *(19 sc)*

Rnd 6: Ch 1, **sc dec** *(see Stitch Guide)* in first 2 sts, [sc dec in next 2 sts] around, ending with sc in last st, join in beg sc. *(10 sc)*

Rnd 7: Ch 1, (sc, ch 3, sc) in first st, ch 3, [(sc, ch 3, sc) in next st, ch 3] around, join in beg sc. Fasten off.

Rep Sleeve in rem armhole.

FINISHING
Sew snap to top edge in back of Gown.

Tack Skirt to Underskirt between sections of ruffles to hold in place.

Sew ribbon roses on Skirt in 8 groups of 2 pink roses with 1 white rose in between around Skirt as shown in photo or as desired.

PANTIES
FRONT
Row 1: Ch 4, sc in 2nd ch from hook and in each ch across, turn. *(3 sc)*

Row 2 (RS): Ch 1, sc in each st across, turn.

Rows 3–10: Ch 1, 2 sc in first st sc in each st across with 2 sc in last st, turn. At end of last row, fasten off. *(19 sc at end of last row)*

BACK
Row 1: With WS facing, working in starting ch on opposite side of row 1 on Front, join with sc in first ch, sc in each of next 2 chs, turn. *(3 sc)*

Row 2 (RS): Ch 1, sc in each st across, turn.

Rows 3–5: Ch 1, 2 sc in first st, sc in each st across, ending with 2 sc in last st, turn. *(9 sc at end of last row)*

Row 6: Working in **front lps** *(see Stitch Guide)*, ch 1, sc in first st, [ch 3, sl st in next st] across, turn.

Row 7: Working in rem lps of row 5, ch 1, 2 sc in first st, sc in each st across, ending with 2 sc in last st, turn. *(11 sc)*

Row 8: Ch 1, 2 sc in first st, sc in each st across, ending with 2 sc in last st, turn. *(13 sc)*

Row 9: Working in front lps, ch 1, sc in first st, [ch 3, sl st in next st] across, turn.

Row 10: Working in rem lps of row 8, ch 1, 2 sc in first st, sc in each st across, ending with 2 sc in last st, turn. *(15 sc)*

Row 11: Ch 1, 2 sc in first st, sc in each st across, ending with 2 sc in last st, turn. *(17 sc)*

Row 12: Working in front lps, ch 1, sc in first st, [ch 3, sl st in next st] across, turn.

Row 13: Working in rem lps of row 11, ch 1, 2 sc in first st, sc in each st across, ending with 2 sc in last st, turn. *(19 sc)*

Rnd 14: Now working in rnds, ch 1, 2 sc in first st, sc in each st across, ending with 2 sc in last st, working in sts across row 10 of Front, sc in each st around, **join** *(see Pattern Notes)* in beg sc. *(40 sc)*

Rnd 15: Ch 1, sc in each st around, join in beg sc. Fasten off.

BOOTIE
MAKE 2.

Rnd 1: Ch 6, 2 sc in 2nd ch from hook, sc in each of next 2 chs, hdc in next ch, 4 hdc in last ch, working on opposite side of ch, hdc in next ch, sc in each of next 2 chs, 2 sc in last ch, **join** (see Pattern Notes) in beg sc. *(14 sc)*

Rnd 2: Ch 1, 2 sc in first st, sc in each of next 3 sts, hdc in next st, 2 hdc in each of next 4 sts, hdc in next st, sc in each of next 3 sts, 2 sc in last st, join in beg sc. *(20 sc)*

Rnd 3: Working in **back lps** (see Stitch Guide), ch 1, sc in first st and in each st around, join in beg sc.

Rnd 4: Working in both lps, ch 1, sc in each of first 7 sts, [**sc dec** (see Stitch Guide) in next 2 sts] 3 times *(toe)*, sc in each of last 7 sts, join in beg sc. *(17 sc)*

Rnd 5: Ch 1, sc in each of first 7 sts, sc dec in next 3 sts, sc in each of last 7 sts, join in beg sc. *(15 sc)*

Rnd 6: Ch 1, sc in each st around, join in beg sc.

Rnd 7: Ch 1, (sc, ch 6, sc) in first st, ch 6, [(sc, ch 6, sc) in next st, ch 6] around, join in beg sc. Fasten off.

Sew 1 pink rose to toe of each Bootie.

HEADBAND

Rnd 1: Ch 32, sl st in first ch to form ring, being careful not to twist ch, mark first ch, ch 1, sc in each ch around, **join** (see Pattern Notes) in beg sc. *(32 sc)*

Rnd 2: Ch 1, sc in each st around, join in beg sc.

TOP EDGING

Ch 1, (sc, ch 6, sc) in first st, ch 6, [(sc, ch 6, sc) in next st, ch 6] 9 times, sc in next st, leaving rem sts unworked. Fasten off.

BOTTOM EDGING

Working on opposite side of starting ch on rnd 1, with WS facing, join with sc in marked ch, ch 6, sc in same st, ch 6, [(sc, ch 6, sc) in next st, ch 6] 9 times, sc in next st, leaving rem sts unworked. Fasten off.

ASSEMBLY

Sew 1 white rose and 2 pink roses to rnds 1 and 2 between Top and Bottom Edgings for front.

Fold tulle widthwise so that 1 end is a little longer than the other. Gather fold and sew to WS of Bottom Edging in back.

BOUQUET

Rnd 1: Ch 2, 6 sc in 2nd ch from hook, **join** (see Pattern Notes) in beg sc. *(6 sc)*

Rnd 2: **Ch 3** (see Pattern Notes), dc in same st, 2 dc in each st around, join in 3rd ch of beg ch-3. *(12 dc)*

Rnd 3: Ch 1, sc in first st, ch 3, [sc in next st, ch 3] around, join in beg sc. Fasten off.

ASSEMBLY

Fold ribbon in half and sew fold in center on RS of Bouquet. Trim ends.

Thread beads onto double strand of sewing thread, alternating colors.

Sew ends of strung beads to center of Bouquet with fold extended out between ends of ribbon.

Sew rem 9 ribbon roses to rnds 1 and 2 on RS of Bouquet as shown in photo. ■

Little Groom
Tuxedo

SKILL LEVEL

INTERMEDIATE

FINISHED SIZE
Fits 5-inch baby doll

MATERIALS
- Size 10 crochet cotton (150 yds per ball):
  1 ball black
  1 ball white
- Super fine (fingering) weight yarn:
  ½ oz/88 yds/14g pink
- Size B/1/2.25mm crochet hook
  or size needed to obtain gauge
- Tapestry needle
- Sewing needle
- White sewing thread
- Snaps: 2
- ¼-inch ribbon roses: 2 pink
- Stitch markers

1 SUPER FINE

GAUGE
7 sc = 1 inch; 8 sc rows = 1 inch

PATTERN NOTES
Join with slip stitch as indicated unless
otherwise stated.

Chain-3 at beginning of row or round counts as
first double crochet unless otherwise stated.

Chain-2 at beginning of row or round **does not**
count as first half double crochet unless
otherwise stated.

Do not apply small beads or buttons to doll
clothing that is intended for play by children
ages 3 or less.

INSTRUCTIONS
SUIT
SHIRT
Row 1: Beg at neckline with white, ch 25, 2 sc
in 2nd ch from hook and in each ch across,
turn. *(48 sc)*

Row 2: Ch 1, sc in each st across, turn.

Row 3 (RS): Ch 1, sc in each of first 8 sts, ch 5,
sk next 10 sts *(armhole)*, sc in each of next 12
sts, ch 5, sk next 10 sts *(armhole)*, sc in each of
last 8 sts, turn. *(10 chs, 28 sc)*

Row 4: Ch 1, sc in each st and in each ch across,
turn. *(38 sc)*

Rows 5–7: Ch 1, sc in each st across, turn.
At end of last row, fasten off.

PANTS
Row 8: With WS facing, join black with sc in
first st, sc in each st across, turn.

Row 9: Ch 1, sc in each st across, turn.

Row 10: Rep row 9.

Rnd 11: Now working in rnds, ch 1, sc in each st around, **join** (see Pattern Notes) in beg sc.

Rnds 12–15: Ch 1, sc in each st around, join in beg sc.

FIRST LEG
Rnd 1: Ch 5, sk first 19 sts, join in next st, ch 1, sc in same st and in each of next 18 sc, sc in each of next 5 chs, leaving rem sts unworked, join in beg sc. (24 sc)

Rnds 2–8: Ch 1, sc in each st around, join in beg sc. At end of last rnd, fasten off.

2ND LEG
Rnd 1: Join black with sc in first unworked st on rnd 15 of Pants, sc in each st and in each ch around, join in beg sc.

Rnds 2–8: Ch 1, sc in each st around, join in beg sc. At end of last rnd, fasten off.

Sew 1 snap to top edge of back opening.

BOWTIE
With pink, ch 5, sc in 2nd ch from hook and in each of next 2 chs, 4 sc in last ch, working on opposite side of ch, sc in each of next 2 chs, 3 sc in last ch, join in beg sc. Fasten off.

Wrap strand pink about 10 times around center of Bowtie. Attach to center front of Shirt as shown in photo.

CUMMERBUND
Row 1: With pink, ch 41, sc in 2nd ch from hook and in each ch across, turn. (40 sc)

Row 2: Working in **back lps** (see Stitch Guide), ch 1, sc in each st across, turn.

Row 3: Working in **front lps** (see Stitch Guide), ch 1, sc in each st across. Fasten off.

Sew rem snap to ends.

JACKET
BODY
Row 1 (RS): Beg at bottom edge with black, ch 42, hdc in 3rd ch from hook and in each ch across, mark last ch, turn. (40 hdc)

Row 2: **Ch 2** (see Pattern Notes), hdc in first st and in each st across, turn.

Rows 3 & 4: Rep row 2.

RIGHT FRONT
Row 1: Ch 2, **hdc dec** (see Stitch Guide) in first 2 sts, hdc in each of next 7 sts, leaving rem sts unworked, turn. (8 hdc)

Row 2: Ch 2, hdc in first st and in each of next 5 sts, hdc dec in last 2 sts, turn. (7 hdc)

Row 3: Ch 2, hdc dec in first 2 sts, hdc in each st across, turn. (6 hdc)

Row 4: Ch 2, hdc in first st and in each of next 3 sts, hdc dec in last 2 sts, turn. (5 hdc)

Row 5: Ch 2, hdc dec in first 2 sts, hdc in each st across, turn. (4 hdc)

Row 6: Ch 2, hdc in first st and in next st, hdc dec in last 2 sts. Leaving long end, fasten off. (3 hdc)

BACK
Row 1: With RS facing, join black in next unworked st on row 4 of Body on Jacket, ch 2, hdc in same st and in each of next 21 sts, leaving rem sts unworked, turn. (22 hdc)

Rows 2–6: Ch 2, hdc in first st and in each st across, turn. At end of last row, fasten off.

LEFT FRONT
Row 1: With RS facing, join black in next unworked st on row 4 of Body on Jacket, ch 2, hdc in same st and in each of next 6 sts, hdc dec in last 2 sts, turn. (8 hdc)

Row 2: Ch 2, hdc dec in first 2 sts, hdc in each st across, turn. (7 hdc)

Row 3: Ch 2, hdc in first st and in each of next 4 sts, hdc dec in last 2 sts, turn. (6 hdc)

Row 4: Ch 2, hdc dec in first 2 sts, hdc in each st across, turn. (5 hdc)

Row 5: Ch 2, hdc in first st and in each of next 2 sts, hdc dec in last 2 sts, turn. (4 hdc)

Row 6: Ch 2, hdc dec in first 2 sts, hdc in each of last 2 sts. Leaving long end, fasten off. *(3 hdc)*

With RS tog, sew shoulder seams.

Turn RS out.

EDGING
With RS facing, working in starting ch on opposite side of row 1 on Body and in ends of rows, join black with sc in marked ch, sc in each ch across with 2 sc in last ch, sc in end of next 4 rows, sc in next row, mark this row for Collar, sc in end of next 4 rows, 2 sc in shoulder seam, sc in each of next 16 sts, 2 sc in shoulder seam, sc in end of next 5 rows, sc in end of next row, mark this row for Collar, sc in end of next 4 rows, sc in same ch as beg sc, join in beg sc. Fasten off.

COLLAR
Working in front lps, join black in marked sc on Edging, sc in next st, hdc in next st, 2 dc in each of next 27 sts, hdc in next st, sc in next st, sl st in next marked st. Fasten off.

Fold Collar back so it lies against Jacket.

Sew 1 rose to Collar as shown in photo.

SLEEVE
Rnd 1: Join black with sc in end of first row on Back at Body, evenly sp 13 sc around, join in beg sc. *(14 sc)*

Rnds 2–4: Ch 2, hdc in first st and in each st around, join in beg hdc. At end of last rnd, fasten off.

Rep Sleeve in rem armhole.

BOOTIE
MAKE 2.
Rnd 1: With black, ch 6, 2 sc in 2nd ch from hook, sc in each of next 2 chs, hdc in next ch, 4 hdc in last ch, working on opposite side of ch, hdc in next ch, sc in each of next 2 chs, 2 sc in last ch, **join** *(see Pattern Notes)* in beg sc. *(14 sts)*

Rnd 2: Ch 1, 2 sc in first st, sc in each of next 3 sts, hdc in next st, 2 hdc in each of next 4 sts, hdc in next st, sc in each of next 3 sts, 2 sc in last st, join in beg sc. *(20 sts)*

Rnd 3: Ch 1, sc in each st around, join in beg sc.

Rnd 4: Ch 1, sc in each of first 7 sts, [**sc dec** *(see Stitch Guide)* in next 2 sts] 3 times *(toe)*, sc in each st around, join in beg sc. *(17 sc)*

Rnd 5: Ch 1, sc in each of first 7 sts, sc dec in next 3 sts, sc in each of last 7 sts, join in beg sc. Fasten off.

Rnd 6: Working in **back lps** *(see Stitch Guide)*, join white with sc in first st, sc in each st around, join in beg sc.

Rnd 7: Ch 1, sc in each st around, join in beg sc. Fasten off.

TOP HAT

Rnd 1: With black, ch 2, 6 sc in 2nd ch from hook, join in beg sc. *(6 sc)*

Rnd 2: Ch 3 *(see Pattern Notes)*, dc in same st, 2 dc in each st around, **join** *(see Pattern Notes)* in 3rd ch of beg ch-3. *(12 dc)*

Rnd 3: Ch 3, dc in same st, 2 dc in each st around, join in 3rd ch of beg ch-3. *(24 dc)*

Rnd 4: Ch 1, sc in first st, 2 sc in next st, [sc in next st, 2 sc in next st] around, join in beg sc. *(36 sc)*

Rnd 5: Working in **back lps** *(see Stitch Guide)*, ch 1, sc in each st around, join in beg sc.

Rnds 6–10: Ch 1, sc in each st around, join in beg sc. At end of last rnd, fasten off.

Rnd 11: Join white with sc in any st, sc in each st around, join in beg sc.

Rnds 12–14: Ch 1, sc in each st around, join in beg sc. At end of last rnd, fasten off.

Rnd 15: Working in **front lps** *(see Stitch Guide)*, join black in any st, ch 3, dc in each st around, join in 3rd ch of beg ch-3. Fasten off.

Sew rose to white section of Top Hat as shown in photo. ■

Lemon-Drop **Dress**

SKILL LEVEL

INTERMEDIATE

FINISHED SIZE
Fits 5-inch baby doll

MATERIALS
- Super fine (fingering) weight yarn:
  2 oz/350 yds/57g yellow
  1 oz/175 yds/28g white
- Size B/1/2.25mm crochet hook or size needed to obtain gauge
- Tapestry needle
- Sewing needle
- Matching sewing thread
- Snap
- ¼-inch ribbon roses: 2 white

SUPER FINE

GAUGE
7 sc = 1 inch; 8 sc rows = 1 inch

PATTERN NOTES
Join with slip stitch as indicated unless otherwise stated.

Chain-3 at beginning of row or round counts as first double crochet unless otherwise stated.

Chain-4 at beginning of row or round counts as first double crochet and chain-1 unless otherwise stated.

Do not apply small beads or buttons to doll clothing that is intended for play by children ages 3 or less.

INSTRUCTIONS
DRESS
Row 1: Beg at neckline with yellow, ch 25, 2 sc in 2nd ch from hook and in each ch across, turn. *(48 sc)*

Row 2 (RS): Ch 1, sc in each of first 8 sts, ch 5, sk next 10 sts *(armhole)*, sc in each of next 12 sts, ch 5, sk next 10 sts *(armhole)*, sc in each of last 8 sts, turn. *(10 chs, 28 sc)*

Row 3: Ch 1, sc in each st and in each ch across, turn. *(38 sc)*

Row 4: Ch 1, sc in each st across, turn.

SKIRT
Row 5: Ch 4 *(see Pattern Notes)*, dc in same st, (dc, ch 1, dc) in each st across, turn.

Rows 6 & 7: Sl st in first ch sp, ch 4, dc in same ch sp, (dc, ch 1, dc) in each ch sp across, turn.

Rnd 8: Now working in rnds, ch 4, dc in same ch sp, (dc, ch 1, dc) in each ch sp around, **join** *(see Pattern Notes)* in 3rd ch of beg ch-4.

Rnds 9 & 10: Sl st in first ch sp, ch 4, dc in same ch sp, (dc, ch 1, dc) in each ch sp around, join in 3rd ch of beg ch-4.

Rnd 11: Sk all ch sps, ch 4, dc in same st, (dc, ch 1, dc) in each st around, join in 3rd ch of beg ch-4. Fasten off.

EDGING
Join white with sc in first st, ch 1, dc in same st, sk next ch sp, (sc, ch 1, dc) in next st, sk all ch sps, (sc, ch 1, dc) in each st around, join in beg sc. Fasten off.

SLEEVE
Rnd 1: Join yellow with sc in center ch of ch-5 at armhole, sc in each of next 2 chs, 2 sc in end of next row, sc in each of next 10 sts, 2 sc in end of next row, sc in each of last 2 chs, join in beg sc. *(19 sc)*

Rnd 2: Ch 4, dc in same st, (dc, ch 1, dc) in each st around, join in 3rd ch of beg ch-4.

Rnd 3: Sl st in first ch sp, ch 1, sc in same ch sp, sc in each ch sp around, join in beg sc. *(19 sc)*

Rnd 4: Ch 1, **sc dec** *(see Stitch Guide)* in first 2 sts, [sc dec in next 2 sts] around, sc in last st, join in beg sc. Fasten off. *(10 sc)*

EDGING
Join white in first st, ch 3 *(does not count as first dc)*, [sl st in next st, ch 3] around, join in beg sl st. Fasten off.

Rep Sleeve and Edging in rem armhole.

Sew snap to top edge of back opening.

Sew 1 rose to center front of Dress.

PANTIES
FRONT
Row 1: With yellow, ch 4, sc in 2nd ch from hook and in each ch across, turn. *(3 sc)*

Row 2 (RS): Ch 1, sc in each st across, turn.

Rows 3–8: Ch 1, 2 sc in first st, sc in each st across with 2 sc in last st, turn. At end of last row, fasten off. *(15 sc at end of last row)*

BACK

Row 1: With WS facing and yellow, working in starting ch on opposite side of row 1 on Front, join with sc in first ch, sc in each of next 2 chs, turn. *(3 sc)*

Rows 2–7: Rep rows 2–7 of Front. *(13 sc at end of last row)*

Rows 8 & 9: Ch 1, 2 sc in first st, sc in each st across with 2 sc in last st, turn. *(17 sc at end of last row)*

Rnd 10: Now working in rnds, ch 1, 2 sc in first st, sc in each st across with 2 sc in last st, working in sts across row 8 of Front, sc in each st around, **join** *(see Pattern Notes)* in beg sc. *(38 sc)*

Rnd 11: Ch 1, sc in each st around, join in beg sc. At end of last rnd, fasten off.

BOOTIE
MAKE 2.

Rnd 1: With yellow, ch 6, 2 sc in 2nd ch from hook, sc in each of next 2 chs, hdc in next ch, 4 hdc in last ch, working on opposite side of ch, hdc in next ch, sc in each of next 2 chs, 2 sc in last ch, **join** *(see Pattern Notes)* in beg sc. *(14 sts)*

Rnd 2: Ch 1, 2 sc in first st, sc in each of next 3 sts, hdc in next st, 2 hdc in each of next 4 sts, hdc in next st, sc in each of next 3 sts, 2 sc in last st, join in beg sc. *(20 sts)*

Rnd 3: Working in **back lps** *(see Stitch Guide)*, ch 1, sc in first st and in each st around, join in beg sc.

Rnd 4: Working in both lps, ch 1, sc in each of first 7 sts, [**sc dec** *(see Stitch Guide)* in next 2 sts] 3 times *(toe)*, sc in each of last 7 sts, join in beg sc. *(17 sc)*

Rnd 5: Ch 1, sc in each of first 7 sts, sc dec in next 3 sts, sc in each of last 7 sts, join in beg sc. *(15 sc)*

Rnds 6 & 7: Ch 1, sc in each st around, join in beg sc. At end of last rnd. Fasten off.

EDGING
Join white in first st, ch 3, [sl st in next st, ch 3] around, join in beg sc. Fasten off.

HAT

Rnd 1: With yellow, ch 4, 9 dc in 4th ch from hook *(first 3 chs count as first dc)*, **join** *(see Pattern Notes)* in 4th ch of beg ch-4. *(10 dc)*

Rnd 2: **Ch 3** *(see Pattern Notes)*, dc in same st, 2 dc in each st around, join in 3rd ch of beg ch-3. *(20 dc)*

Rnd 3: Ch 3, dc in same st, dc in next st, [2 dc in next st, dc in next st] around, join in 3rd ch of beg ch-3. *(30 dc)*

Rnds 4 & 5: Ch 3, dc in each st around, join in 3rd ch of beg ch-3.

Rnd 6: **Ch 4** *(see Pattern Notes)*, dc in same st, (dc, ch 1, dc) in each st around, join in 3rd ch of beg ch-4. Fasten off.

EDGING
Join white in first st, ch 3 *(does not count as first dc)*, [sl st in next st, ch 3] around, join in beg sl st. Fasten off.

Sew rem rose to Hat as shown in photo. ∎

Pistachio
Party Dress

SKILL LEVEL

INTERMEDIATE

FINISHED SIZE
Fits 5-inch baby doll

MATERIALS
- Super fine (fingering) weight yarn: 1¾ oz/306 yds/50g each pink, green and white
- Size B/1/2.25mm crochet hook or size needed to obtain gauge
- Tapestry needle
- Sewing needle
- Matching sewing thread
- Snap
- ¼-inch ribbon roses: 2 pink

SUPER FINE

GAUGE
7 sc = 1 inch; 8 sc rows = 1 inc

PATTERN NOTES
Join with slip stitch as indicated unless otherwise stated.

Chain-3 at beginning of row or round counts as first double crochet unless otherwise stated.

Chain-4 at beginning of row or round counts as first double crochet and chain-1 unless otherwise stated.

Do not apply small beads or buttons to doll clothing that is intended for play by children ages 3 or less.

INSTRUCTIONS
DRESS
Row 1: Beg at neckline with pink, ch 25, 2 sc in 2nd ch from and in each ch across, turn. *(48 sc)*

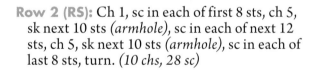

Row 2 (RS): Ch 1, sc in each of first 8 sts, ch 5, sk next 10 sts *(armhole)*, sc in each of next 12 sts, ch 5, sk next 10 sts *(armhole)*, sc in each of last 8 sts, turn. *(10 chs, 28 sc)*

Row 3: Ch 1, sc each st and in each ch across, turn. *(38 sc)*

Row 4: Ch 1, sc in each st across, turn.

SKIRT
Row 5: Ch 3 *(see Pattern Notes)*, dc in first st, 2 dc in each st around, join in 3rd ch of beg ch-3. *(76 dc)*

Row 6: Working in **front lps** *(see Stitch Guide)*, **ch 4** *(see Pattern Notes)*, dc in same st, [ch 1, (dc, ch 1, dc) in next st] across, turn. Fasten off. *(152 dc)*

Row 7: With WS facing and neckline pointed down, working in rem lps of row 5, **join** *(see Pattern Notes)* green in first st, ch 3, dc in same st, dc in each st across, ending with 2 dc in last st, turn. *(78 dc)*

Rnd 8: Now working in rnds, ch 3, dc in same st, dc in next st, [2 dc in next st, dc in next st] around, join in 3rd ch of beg ch-3. *(117 dc)*

Rnd 9: Working in front lps, ch 4, dc in same st, ch 1, [(dc, ch 1, dc) in next st, ch 1] around, join in 3rd ch of beg ch-4. Fasten off.

Rnd 10: Working in rem lps of rnd 8, join pink in any st, ch 3, dc in each st around, join in 3rd ch of beg ch-3. *(117 dc)*

Rnd 11: Ch 3, dc in each st around, join in 3rd ch of beg ch-3.

Rnd 12: Ch 4, dc in same st, ch 1, [(dc, ch 1, dc) in next st, ch 1] around, join in 3rd ch of beg ch-4. Fasten off.

Sew snap to top edge of back opening.

Sew 1 rose to center front as shown in photo.

HEADBAND

Rnd 1: With green, ch 32, sl st in first ch to form ring, being careful not to twist ch, ch 1, sc in each ch around, **join** *(see Pattern Notes)* in beg sc. *(32 sc)*

Rnd 2: Ch 1, sc in each st around, join in beg sc. Fasten off.

EDGING

Join pink in any st, ch 3, [sl st in next st, ch 3] around, join in beg sl st. Fasten off.

Working in starting ch on opposite side of rnd 1, join pink in any st, ch 3, [sl st in next st, ch 3] around, join in beg sl st. Fasten off.

Sew rose in center of Headband.

PANTIES
FRONT

Row 1: With pink, ch 4, sc in 2nd ch from hook and in each ch across, turn. *(3 sc)*

Row 2 (RS): Ch 1, sc in each st across, turn.

Rows 3–8: Ch 1, 2 sc in first st, sc in each st across with 2 sc in last st, turn. At end of last row, fasten off. *(15 sc at end of last row)*

BACK

Row 1: With WS facing and working in starting ch on opposite side of row 1 on Front, join pink with sc in first ch, sc in each of next 2 chs, turn. *(3 sc)*

Rows 2–7: Rep rows 2–7 of Front. *(13 sc at end of last row)*

Rows 8 & 9: Ch 1, 2 sc in first st, sc in each st across with 2 sc in last st, turn. *(17 sc at end of last row)*

Rnd 10: Now working in rnds, ch 1, 2 sc in first st, sc in each st across with 2 sc in last st, with WS tog, sc in each st across Front, **join** *(see Pattern Notes)* in beg sc.

Rnd 11: Ch 1, sc in each st around, join in beg sc. Fasten off.

BOOTIE
MAKE 2.

Rnd 1: With pink, ch 6, 2 sc in 2nd ch from hook, sc in each of next 2 chs, hdc in next ch, 4 hdc in last ch, working on opposite side of ch, hdc in next ch, sc in each of next 2 chs, 2 sc in last ch, **join** *(see Pattern Notes)* in beg sc. *(14 sc)*

Rnd 2: Ch 1, 2 sc in first st, sc in each of next 3 sts, hdc in next st, 2 hdc in each of next 4 sts, hdc in next st, sc in each of next 3 sts, 2 sc in last st, join in beg sc. *(20 sc)*

Rnd 3: Working in **back lps** *(see Stitch Guide)*, ch 1, sc in first st and in each st around, join in beg sc.

Rnd 4: Working in both lps, ch 1, sc in each of first 7 sts, [**sc dec** *(see Stitch Guide)* in next 2 sts] 3 times *(toe)*, sc in each of last 7 sts, join in beg sc. Fasten off. *(17 sc)*

SOCK

Rnd 5: Working in back lps, join white with sc in first st, sc in each of next 6 sts, sc dec in next 3 sts, sc in each of last 7 sts, join in beg sc. *(15 sc)*

Rnd 6: Ch 1, sc in each st around, join in beg sc.

Rnd 7: **Ch 3** *(see Pattern Notes)*, dc in same st, and in each st around, join in 3rd ch of beg ch-3. Fasten off.

STRAP

Working in rem lps on rnd 4, join pink with sc in first st, sc in each of next 3 sts, ch 8, sk next 9 sts, sc in each of last 4 sts, join in beg sc. Fasten off. ∎

Peaches & Cream

SKILL LEVEL

INTERMEDIATE

FINISHED SIZE
Fits 5-inch baby doll

MATERIALS

- Super fine (fingering) weight yarn:
  1¾ oz/306 yds/50g peach
  ½ oz/88 yds/14g cream
- Size B/1/2.25mm crochet hook
  or size needed to obtain gauge
- Size 6/1.80mm steel crochet hook
- Tapestry needle
- Sewing needle
- Matching sewing thread
- Snap
- Tiny buttons: 2

1 SUPER FINE

GAUGE
7 sc = 1 inch; 8 sc rows = 1 inch

PATTERN NOTES
Use size B hook unless otherwise stated.

Join with slip stitch as indicated unless
otherwise stated.

Chain-3 at beginning of row or round counts as
first double crochet unless otherwise stated.

Do not apply small beads or buttons to doll
clothing that is intended for play by children
ages 3 or less.

INSTRUCTIONS
DRESS
Row 1: Beg at neck, with **size B hook** *(see
Pattern Notes)* and cream, ch 25, 2 sc in 2nd ch
from hook and in each ch across, turn. *(48 sc)*

Row 2 (RS): Ch 1, sc in each of first 8 sts, ch 5,
sk next 10 sts *(armhole)*, sc in each of next 12
sts, ch 5, sk next 10 sts *(armhole)*, sc in each of
last 8 sts, turn. *(10 chs, 28 sc)*

Row 3: Ch 1, sc in each st and in each ch across, turn. *(38 sc)*

Row 4: Ch 1, sc st across, turn. Fasten off.

Row 5: With WS facing, **join** *(see Pattern Notes)* peach in first st, **ch 3** *(see Pattern Notes)*, dc in same st, 2 dc in each st across, turn. *(76 dc)*

Row 6: Ch 3, dc in each st across. Fasten off.

EDGING
Join cream with sc in first st, sk next st, 4 dc in next st, [sk next st, sc in next st, sk next st, 4 dc in next st] across, ending with sc in last st. Fasten off.

Sew snap to top edge of back opening.

FLOWER
MAKE 2.
With size 6 steel hook and peach, ch 3, sl st in 3rd ch from hook, [ch 2, sl st in same ch] 5 times. Leaving long end, fasten off.

Sew 1 Flower to front of Dress as shown in photo. Set rem Flower aside. Sew 1 button to center of Flower.

SHORTS
Rnd 1 (RS): With peach, ch 28, sl st in first ch to form ring, being careful not to twist ch, ch 1, sc in each ch around, **join** *(see Pattern Notes)* in beg sc. *(28 sc)*

Rnds 2–8: Ch 1, sc in each st around, join in beg sc.

FIRST LEG
Ch 4, sk next 13 sts, sl st in next st, sc in same st, sc in each of next 13 sts, sc in each of next 4 chs, leaving rem sts unworked, join in beg sc. Fasten off. *(18 sc)*

EDGING
Join cream with sc in any st, 3 dc in next st, [sc in next st, 3 dc in next st] around, join in beg sc. Fasten off.

2ND LEG
Join peach with sc in joining on rnd 8, sc in each of next 13 unworked sts on rnd 8 of Shorts, sc in each of next 4 chs, join in beg sc. Fasten off.

EDGING
Join cream with sc in any st, 3 dc in next st, [sc in next st, 3 dc in next st] around, join in beg sc. Fasten off.

BOOTIE
MAKE 2.
Rnd 1: With peach, ch 6, 2 sc in 2nd ch from hook, sc in each of next 2 chs, hdc in next ch, 4 hdc in last ch, working on opposite side of ch, hdc in next ch, sc in each of next 2 chs, 2 sc in last ch, **join** *(see Pattern Notes)* in beg sc. *(14 sts)*

Rnd 2: Ch 1, 2 sc in first st, sc in each of next 3 sts, hdc in next st, 2 hdc in each of next 4 sts *(toe)*, hdc in next st, sc in each of next 3 sts, 2 sc in last st, join in beg sc. *(20 sts)*

Rnd 3: Ch 1, sc in each st around, join in beg sc.

Rnd 4: Ch 1, sc in each of first 7 sts, [**sc dec** *(see Stitch Guide)* in next 2 sts] 3 times, sc in each of last 7 sts, join in beg sc. *(17 sc)*

Rnd 5: Ch 1, sc in each of first 4 sts, ch 8, sk next 9 sts, sc in each of last 4 sts, join in beg sc. Fasten off.

HEADBAND
Rnd 1: With cream, ch 34, sl st in first ch to form ring, being careful not to twist ch, ch 1, sc in each ch around, **join** *(see Pattern Notes)* in beg sc. *(34 sc)*

Rnd 2: Ch 1, sc in each st around, join in beg sc.

Rnd 3: Rep rnd 2. Fasten off.

Sew rem Flower to Headband and sew button in center of Flower. ∎

Lavender & Rose
Sundress

SKILL LEVEL

INTERMEDIATE

FINISHED SIZE
Fits 5-inch baby doll

MATERIALS
- Super fine (fingering) weight yarn: 1 oz/175 yds/28g each lilac and antique white
- Size B/1/2.25mm crochet hook or size needed to obtain gauge
- Tapestry needle
- Sewing needle
- Matching sewing thread
- Snap
- ¼-inch lavender ribbon roses: 2

1 SUPER FINE

GAUGE
7 sc = 1 inch; 8 sc rows = 1 inch

PATTERN NOTES
Join with slip stitch as indicated unless otherwise stated.

Chain-3 at beginning of row or round counts as first double crochet unless otherwise stated.

Do not apply small beads or buttons to doll clothing that is intended for play by children ages 3 or less.

INSTRUCTIONS
DRESS
Row 1: Beg at neckline with antique white, ch 25, 2 sc in 2nd ch from hook and in each ch across, turn. (48 sc)

Row 2 (RS): Ch 1, sc in each of first 8 sts, ch 5, sk next 10 sts (armhole), sc in each of next 12 sts, ch 5, sk next 10 sts (armhole), sc in each of last 8 sts, turn. (10 chs, 28 sc)

Row 3: Ch 1, sc in each st and in each ch across, turn. (38 sc)

Row 4: Ch 1, sc in each st across, turn.

Row 5: Working in **back lps** (see Stitch Guide), ch 1, sc in first st, [ch 1, sc in next st] across. Fasten off.

SKIRT
Row 6: With RS facing and working in rem lps on row 4, join lilac with sc in first st, 5 dc in next st, [sc in next st, 5 dc in next st] across, turn.

Row 7: Sl st in each of next 2 dc, ch 1, sc in next dc, sk next 2 dc, 5 dc in next sc, [sk next 2 dc, sc in next dc, sk next 2 dc, 5 dc in next sc] across, turn.

Rnd 8: Now working in rnds, sl st in each of first 2 dc, ch 1, sc in next dc, sk next 2 dc, *5 dc in next sc**, sk next 2 dc, sc in next dc, sk next 2 dc, rep from * around, ending last rep at **, **join** (see Pattern Notes) in beg sc.

Rnd 9: **Ch 3** (*see Pattern Notes*), 2 dc in same st, sk next 2 dc, sc in next dc, [sk next 2 dc, 5 dc in next sc, sk next 2 dc, sc in next dc] around, sk last 2 dc, 2 dc in same st as beg ch-3, join in 3rd ch of beg ch-3.

Rnd 10: Ch 1, sc in first st, *sk next 2 dc, 5 dc in next sc, sk next 2 dc**, sc in next dc, rep from * around, ending last rep at **, join in beg sc.

Rnds 11 & 12: Rep rnds 9 and 10. At end of last rnd, fasten off.

Sew snap to top edge of back opening.

Sew 1 rose to center front.

BLOOMERS
Rnd 1: Beg at waist with lilac, ch 28, sl st in first ch to form ring, being careful not to twist ch, ch 3, dc in each ch around, **join** (*see Pattern Notes*) in 3rd ch of beg ch-3. (*28 dc*)

Rnds 2–4: **Ch 3** (*see Pattern Notes*), dc in each st around, join in beg ch-3.

FIRST LEG
Ch 3, sk next 13 sts, sl st in next st, ch 3, dc in each of last 13 sts, dc in each of first 3 chs, join in 3rd ch of beg ch-3. Fasten off. (*17 dc*)

EDGING
Join antique white with sc in any st, ch 1, [sc in next st, ch 1] around, join in beg sc. Fasten off.

2ND LEG
Join lilac in first sk st on rnd 4 of Bloomers, ch 3, dc in each st and in each ch around, join in 3rd ch of beg ch-3. Fasten off.

EDGING
Join antique white with sc in any st, ch 1, [sc in next st, ch 1] around, join in beg sc. Fasten off.

BOOTIE
MAKE 2.
Rnd 1: With lilac, ch 6, 2 sc in 2nd ch from hook, sc in each of next 2 chs, hdc in next ch, 4 hdc in last ch, working on opposite side of ch, hdc in next ch, sc in each of next 2 chs, 2 sc in last ch, **join** (*see Pattern Notes*) in beg sc. (*14 sc*)

Rnd 2: Ch 1, 2 sc in first st, sc in each of next 3 sts, hdc in next st, 2 hdc in each of next 4 sts, hdc in next st, sc in each of next 3 sts, 2 sc in last st, join in beg sc. (*20 sc*)

Rnd 3: Working in **back lps** (*see Stitch Guide*), ch 1, sc in first st and in each st around, join in beg sc.

Rnd 4: Working in both lps, ch 1, sc in each of first 7 sts, [**sc dec** (*see Stitch Guide*) in next 2 sts] 3 times (*toe*), sc in each of last 7 sts, join in beg sc. Fasten off. (*17 sc*)

SOCK
Rnd 5: Working in back lps, join antique white with sc in first st, sc in each of next 6 sts, sc dec in next 3 sts, sc in each of last 7 sts, join in beg sc. (*15 sc*)

Rnd 6: Ch 1, sc in each st around, join in beg sc.

Rnd 7: **Ch 3** (*see Pattern Notes*), dc in same st, and in each st around, join in 3rd ch of beg ch-3. Fasten off.

STRAP
Working in rem lps on rnd 4, join soft lilac with sc in first st, sc in each of next 3 sts, ch 8, sk next 9 sts, sc in each of last 4 sts, join in beg sc. Fasten off.

HAT
Rnd 1: With antique white, ch 4, 9 dc in 4th ch from hook (*first 3 chs count as first dc*), **join** (*see Pattern Notes*) in 4th ch of beg ch-4. (*10 dc*)

Rnd 2: **Ch 3** (*see Pattern Notes*), dc in same st, 2 dc in each st around, join in 3rd ch of beg ch-3. (*20 dc*)

Rnd 3: Rep rnd 2. (*40 dc*)

Rnds 4 & 5: Ch 3, dc in each st around, join in 3rd ch of beg ch-3.

Rnd 6: Ch 1, sc in each of first 9 sts, **sc dec** (*see Stitch Guide*) in next 2 sts, [sc in each of next 9 sts, sc dec in next 2 sts] twice, sc in each of last 7 sts, join in beg sc. Fasten off. (*37 sc*)

EDGING
Join lilac with sc in any st, ch 1, [sc in next st, ch 1] around, join in beg sc. Fasten off.

Sew rose to center front of Hat. ∎

Little Miss
Two-Piece Romper

SKILL LEVEL

INTERMEDIATE

FINISHED SIZE
Fits 5-inch baby doll

MATERIALS
- Super fine (fingering) weight yarn: 1 oz/175 yds/28g each plum and cream
- Size B/1/2.25mm crochet hook or size needed to obtain gauge
- Tapestry needle
- Sewing needle
- White sewing thread
- Snap
- Small white ribbon roses: 2

1 SUPER FINE

GAUGE
7 sc = 1 inch; 8 sc rows = 1 inch

PATTERN NOTES
Join with slip stitch as indicated unless otherwise stated.

Chain-3 at beginning of row or round counts as first double crochet unless otherwise stated.

Do not apply small beads or buttons to doll clothing that is intended for play by children ages 3 or less.

INSTRUCTIONS
DRESS
Row 1: Beg at neck with plum, ch 25, 2 sc in 2nd ch from hook and in each ch across, turn. *(48 sc)*

Row 2 (RS): Ch 1, sc in each of first 8 sts, ch 5, sk next 10 sts *(armhole)*, sc in each of next 12 sts, ch 5, sk next 10 sts *(armhole)*, sc in each of last 8 sts, turn. *(10 chs, 28 sc)*

Row 3: Ch 1, sc in each st and in each ch across, turn. *(38 sc)*

Row 4: Ch 1, sc in each st across, turn. Fasten off.

SKIRT
Row 5: With WS facing, **join** (*see Pattern Notes*) cream in first st, **ch 3** (*see Pattern Notes*), (dc, ch 1, 2 dc) in same st, [sk next st, (2 dc, ch 1, 2 dc) in next st] across, leaving last st unworked, turn.

Row 6: Sl st in each of first 2 sts and in ch sp, ch 3, (dc, ch 1, 2 dc) in same ch sp, (2 dc, ch 1, 2 dc) in each ch-1 sp across, turn.

Row 7: Rep row 6. Fasten off.

Row 8: Join plum in first ch-1 sp, ch 3, 6 dc in same ch sp, 7 dc in each ch-1 sp across. Fasten off.

SLEEVE
Rnd 1: Join cream in center ch of ch-5 on armhole, ch 3, dc in each of next 2 chs, 2 dc in end of next row, 2 dc in each of next 10 sts, 2 sc in end of next row, dc in each of last 2 chs, join in 3rd ch of beg ch-3. (*29 dc*)

Rnd 2: Ch 1, **sc dec** (*see Stitch Guide*) in first 2 sts, [sc dec in next 2 sts] around, ending with sc in last st, join in beg sc. (*15 sc*)

Rnd 3: Ch 1, sc in each st around, join in beg sc. Fasten off.

EDGING
Join plum in first st, ch 2, [sl st in next st, ch 2] around, join in beg sl st. Fasten off.

Rep Sleeve in rem armhole.

Sew snap to top edge of back opening.

Sew 1 rose to center front of Dress.

PANTS
Rnd 1 (RS): With cream, ch 32, sl st in first ch to form ring, being careful not to twist ch, ch 3, dc in same ch, dc in next ch, [2 dc in next ch, dc in next ch] around, **join** (*see Pattern Notes*) in 3rd ch of beg ch-3. (*48 dc*)

Rnds 2 & 3: Ch 3 (*see Pattern Notes*), dc in each st around, join in 3rd ch of beg ch-3.

FIRST LEG
Rnd 1: Ch 2, sk next 23 sts, join in next st, ch 3, dc in each st around, dc in each of next 2 chs, join in 3rd ch of beg ch-3. (*26 dc*)

Rnds 2 & 3: Ch 3, dc in each st around, join in 3rd ch of beg ch-3.

Rnd 4: Ch 1, **sc dec** (*see Stitch Guide*) in first 2 sts, [sc dec in next2 sts] around, join in beg sc. (*13 sc*)

Rnd 5: Ch 1, sc in each st around, join in beg sc. Fasten off.

EDGING
Join plum in any st, ch 1, [sl st in next st, ch 1] around, join in beg sl st. Fasten off.

2ND LEG
Rnd 1: Working in sk sts on rnd 3 of Pants, join cream in first st, ch 3, dc in each sk st around, join in 3rd ch of beg ch-3.

Rnds 2–5: Rep rnds 1–5 of First Leg.

EDGING
Join plum in any st, ch 1, [sl st in next st, ch 1] around, join in beg sl st. Fasten off.

BOOTIE
MAKE 2.
Rnd 1: With plum, ch 6, 2 sc in 2nd ch from hook, sc in each of next 2 chs, hdc in next ch, 4 hdc in last ch, working on opposite side of ch, hdc in next ch, sc in each of next 2 chs, 2 sc in last ch, join in beg sc. (*14 sc*)

Rnd 2: Ch 1, 2 sc in first st, sc in each of next 3 sts, hdc in next st, 2 hdc in each of next 4 sts, hdc in next st, sc in each of next 3 sts, 2 sc in last st, join in beg sc. (*20 sc*)

Rnd 3: Working in **back lps** (*see Stitch Guide*), ch 1, sc in first st and in each st around, join in beg sc.

Rnd 4: Working in **both lps**, ch 1, sc in each of first 7 sts, [**sc dec** (*see Stitch Guide*) in next 2 sts] 3 times (*toe*), sc in each of last 7 sts, join in beg sc. (*17 sc*)

Rnd 5: Ch 1, sc in each of first 4 sts, ch 8, sk next 9 sts, sc in each of last 4 sts, join in beg sc. Fasten off.

HAT
Rnd 1: With plum, ch 4, 9 dc in 4th ch from hook (*first 3 chs count as first dc*), join in 4th ch of beg ch-4. (*10 dc*)

Rnd 2: Ch 3 (*see Pattern Notes*), dc in same st, 2 dc in each st around, join in 3rd ch of beg ch-3. (*20 dc*)

Rnd 3: Rep rnd 2. (*40 dc*)

Rnd 4: Ch 3, dc in same st, dc in next st, [2 dc in next st, dc in next st] around, join in 3rd ch of beg ch-3. (*60 dc*)

Rnd 5: Ch 3, dc in each st around, join in 3rd ch of beg ch-3.

Rnd 6: Ch 1, **sc dec** (*see Stitch Guide*) in first 2 sts, [sc dec in next 2 sts] around, join in beg sc. (*30 sc*)

Rnd 7: Ch 1, sc in each st around, join in beg sc. Fasten off.

EDGING
Join cream with sc in first st, ch 2, [sc in next st, ch 2] around, join in beg sc. Fasten off.

Sew rem rose to Hat as shown in photo. ∎

Winter
Bunting Bag

SKILL LEVEL

INTERMEDIATE

FINISHED SIZE
Fits 5-inch baby doll

MATERIALS
- Super fine (fingering) weight yarn: 3 oz/475 yds/85g yellow
- Size B/1/2.25mm crochet hook or size needed to obtain gauge
- Tapestry needle
- Sewing needle
- Yellow sewing thread
- Small star-shaped buttons: 6

GAUGE
7 sc = 1 inch; 8 sc rows = 1 inch

PATTERN NOTES
Join with slip stitch as indicated unless otherwise stated.

Chain-3 at beginning of row or round counts as first double crochet unless otherwise stated.

Do not apply small beads or buttons to doll clothing that is intended for play by children ages 3 or less.

INSTRUCTIONS
BUNTING BAG

Row 1 (RS): Beg at neckline, ch 21, 2 sc in 2nd ch from hook and in each ch across, turn. *(40 sc)*

Row 2: Ch 1, sc in first st, ch 2, sk next 2 sts *(buttonhole)*, sc in each st across, turn.

Row 3: Ch 1, sc in each of first 6 sts, ch 5, sk next 8 sts *(armhole)*, sc in each of next 12 sts, ch 5, sk next 8 sts *(armhole)*, sc in each of next 3 sts, sc in each of next 2 chs, sc in last st, turn. *(10 chs, 24 sts)*

Row 4: Ch 1, sc in each st and in each ch across, turn. *(34 sc)*

Row 5: Ch 1, sc in each of first 4 sts, 3 dc in next st, [sc in next st, 3 dc in next st] 12 times, sc in each of next 2 sts, ch 2, sk next 2 sts *(buttonhole)*, sc in last st, turn.

Row 6: Ch 1, sc in first st, sc in each of next 2 chs, sc in next st, 2 dc in next st, sk next st, sc in next st, [sk next st, 3 dc in next st, sk next st, sc in next st] 12 times, sk next st, 2 dc in next st, sc in each of last 3 sts, turn.

Row 7: Ch 1, sc in each of first 4 sts, sk next st, 3 dc in next st, [sk next st, sc in next st, sk next st, 3 dc in next st] 12 times, sk next st, sc in each of last 5 sts, turn.

Row 8: Ch 1, sc in first st, ch 2, sk next 2 sts *(buttonhole)*, sc in next st, 2 dc in next st, sk next st, sc in next st, [sk next st, 3 dc in next st, sk next st, sc in next st] 12 times, 2 dc in next st, sc in each of last 3 sts, turn.

Row 9: Ch 1, sc in each of first 4 sts, sk next st, 3 dc in next st, [sk next st, sc in next st, sk next st, 3 dc in next st] 12 times, sk next st, sc in each of next 2 sts, sc in each of next 2 chs, sc in last st, turn.

Row 10: Ch 1, sc in each of first 4 sts, 2 dc in next st, sk next st, sc in next st, [sk next st, 3 dc in next st, sk next st, sc in next st] 12 times, sk next st, 2 dc in next st, sc in each of last 3 sts, turn.

Row 11: Ch 1, sc in each of first 4 sts, sk next st, 3 dc in next st, [sk next st, sc in next st, sk next st, 3 dc in next st] 12 times, sk next st, sc in each of next 2 sts, ch 2, sk next 2 sts *(buttonhole)*, sc in last st, turn.

Row 12: Ch 1, sc in first st and in each of next 2 chs, sc in next st, 2 dc in next st, sk next st, sc in next st, [sk next st, 3 dc in next st, sk next st, sc in next st] 12 times, sk next st, 2 dc in next st, sc in each of last 3 sts, turn.

Rows 13–18: Rep rows 7–12.

Rnd 19: Now working in rnds, overlap first 3 sts *(buttonhole side)* over top of last 3 sts, working through both thicknesses, ch 1, sc in each of first 4 sts, sk next st, 3 dc in next st, [sk next st, sc in next st, sk next st, 3 dc in next st] 12 times, sk next st, sc in each of last 2 sts, **join** *(see Pattern Notes)* in beg sc.

Rnd 20: Sl st in next st, ch 1, sc in same st, sk next st, 3 dc in next st, sk next st, sc in next st, [sk next st, 3 dc in next st, sk next st, sc in next st] 12 times, sk in next st, 3 dc in last st, join in beg sc.

Rnd 21: Ch 3 *(see Pattern Notes)*, 2 dc in same st, sk next st, sc in next st, [sk next st, 3 dc in next st, sk next st, sc in next st] around, join in 3rd ch of beg ch-3.

Rnd 22: Sl st in next st, ch 1, sc in same st, sk next st, 3 dc in next st, [sk next st, sc in next st, sk next st, 3 dc in next st] around, join in beg sc.

BOTTOM

Rnd 23: Ch 1, evenly sp 60 sc around, join in beg sc.

Rnds 24 & 25: Ch 2, dc in next st, [**dc dec** *(see Stitch Guide)* in next 2 sts] around, join in beg dc. *(15 dc at end of last rnd)*

Rnd 26: Ch 1, **ssc dec** *(see Stitch Guide)* in first 3 sts, [sc dec in next 3 sts] around, join in beg sc. Leaving long end, fasten off. *(5 sc)*

Weave long end through top of sts on last rnd, pull to close. Secure end.

SLEEVE

Rnd 1: Join with sc in center ch of ch-5 on armhole, sc in each of next 2 chs, 2 sc in end of next row, sc in each of next 8 sts, sc in end of next row, sc in each of last 2 chs, join in beg sc. *(16 sc)*

Rnd 2: Ch 1, sc in first st, 3 dc in next st, [sc in next st, 3 dc in next st] around, join in beg sc.

Rnd 3: Ch 3, dc in same st, sk next st, sc in next st, [sk next st, 3 dc in next st, sk next st, sc in next st] around, join in 3rd ch of beg ch-3.

Rnd 4: Sl st in next st, ch 1, sc in same st, sk next st, 3 dc in next st, [sk next st, sc in next st, sk next st, 3 dc in next st] around, join in beg sc.

Rnds 5 & 6: Rep rnds 3 and 4.

Rnd 7: Ch 1, sc dec in first 2 sts, [sc dec in next 2 sts] around, join in beg sc. *(16 sc)*

Rnd 8: Ch 1, sc dec in first 2 sts, sc in next st, [sc dec in next 2 sts, sc in next st] around, ending with sc in last st, join in beg sc. *(11 sc)*

Rnd 9: Ch 1, sc in each st around, join in beg sc. Fasten off.

Rep on rem armhole.

HOOD

Row 1: Working in starting ch on opposite side of row 1 on Bunting Bag, with RS facing, join with sc in first ch, sc in each ch across, turn. *(20 sc)*

Row 2: Ch 3, dc in same st, sc in next st, [3 dc in next st, sc in next st] across to last 2 sts, sk next st, 2 dc in last st, turn.

Row 3: Ch 1, sc in first st, [sk next st, 3 dc in next st, sk next st, sc in next st] across, turn.

Row 4: Ch 3, dc in same st, sk next st, sc in next st, [sk next st, 3 dc in next st, sk next st, sc in next st] across, ending with 2 dc in last st, turn.

Rows 5–10: [Rep rows 3 and 4 alternately] 3 times.

Row 11: Rep row 3.

Row 12: Ch 1, sc in each st across, turn. *(37 sc)*

Row 13: Fold last row in half, working through both thicknesses, sl st in each st across. Fasten off.

TRIM

With RS facing, working in ends of rows around front opening, join with sc in end of first row, evenly sp sc across to opposite side. Fasten off.

Sew buttons to front opposite buttonholes. ■

Pretty Princess
Nightgown

OUTFIT
SKILL LEVEL

INTERMEDIATE

FINISHED SIZE
Fits 5-inch baby doll

MATERIALS
- Super fine (fingering) weight yarn:
  2 oz/350 yds/57g white
  1 oz/175 yds/28g pink
- Size B/1/2.25mm crochet hook
  or size needed to obtain gauge
- Tapestry needle
- Sewing needle
- Matching sewing thread
- Snap
- Tiny pearl beads: 2

SUPER FINE

GAUGE
7 sc = 1 inch; 8 sc rows = 1 inch

PATTERN NOTES
Join with slip stitch as indicated unless
  otherwise stated.

Chain-3 at beginning of row or round counts as
  first double crochet unless otherwise stated.

Chain-2 at beginning of row or round **does not**
  count as first stitch unless otherwise stated.

Do not apply small beads or buttons to doll
  clothing that is intended for play by children
  ages 3 or less.

INSTRUCTIONS
GOWN
BODICE

Row 1: Beg at neckline with white, ch 25, 2 sc in 2nd ch from hook and in each ch across, turn. *(48 sc)*

Row 2: Ch 1, sc in each st across, turn.

Row 3 (RS): Ch 1, sc in each of first 8 sts, ch 5, sk next 10 sts *(armhole)*, sc in each of next 12 sts, ch 5, sk next 10 sts *(armhole)*, sc in each of last 8 sts, turn. *(10 chs, 28 sts)*

Row 4: Ch 1, sc in each st and ch across, turn. *(38 sc)*

Row 5: Ch 1, sc in each st across, turn.

SKIRT

Row 6: Working in **front lps** *(see Stitch Guide)*, ch 1, sc in first st, sk next st, 3 dc in next st, sk next st, sc in next st, [sk next st, 3 dc in next st, sk next st, sc in next st] across, leaving last st unworked, turn.

Row 7: Working in **back lps** *(see Stitch Guide)*, **ch 3** *(see Pattern Notes)*, 2 dc in first sc, [sk next dc, sc in next dc, sk next dc, 3 dc in next sc] across, turn.

Row 8: Working in front lps, sl st in first dc, ch 1, sc in next dc, [sk next dc, 3 dc in next sc, sk next dc, sc in next dc] across, turn.

Rnd 9: Now working in rnds and working rem rnds in back lps, ch 3, 2 dc in same st, [sk next dc, sc in next dc, sk next dc, 3 dc in next sc] around, **join** *(see Pattern Notes)* in 3rd ch of beg ch-3.

Rnd 10: Ch 3, 2 dc in same st, sc in next dc, sk next dc, [3 dc in next sc, sk next dc, sc in next dc, sk next dc] around, join in 3rd ch of beg ch-3.

Rnd 11: Sl st in next dc, ch 1, sc in same dc, sk next dc, 3 dc in next sc, sk next dc, [sc in next dc, sk next dc, 3 dc in next sc, sk next dc] around, join in beg sc.

Rnd 12: Ch 3, 2 dc in same st, sk next dc, sc in next dc, sk next dc, [3 dc in next sc, sk next dc, sc in next dc, sk next dc] around, join in 3rd ch of beg ch-3.

Rnds 13 & 14: Rep rnds 11 and 12.

RUFFLE

Rnd 15: Working in both lps, ch 1, evenly sp 40 sc around, join in beg sc. *(40 sc)*

Rnd 16: Working in back lps, ch 3, 2 dc in same st, 2 dc in next st, [3 dc in next st, 2 dc in next st] around, join in 3rd ch of beg ch-3. Fasten off. *(100 dc)*

BODICE EDGING

With RS facing and neckline pointed down, working in rem lps of row 5 of Bodice, join pink in first st, [ch 1, sl st in next st] across. Fasten off.

RUFFLE EDGING

With RS facing and neckline pointed down, working in rem lps of rnd 15 on Ruffle, join pink in first st, ch 1, [sl st in next st, ch 1] around, join in beg sl st. Fasten off.

SLEEVE

Rnd 1: Join white in center ch at armhole, ch 3, dc in each of next 2 chs, 2 dc in end of next row, dc in each of next 10 sts, 2 dc in end of next st, dc in each of last 2 chs, join in 3rd ch of beg ch-3. *(19 dc)*

Rnds 2–4: Ch 3, dc in each st around, join in 3rd ch of beg ch-3.

Rnd 5: Ch 1, **sc dec** *(see Stitch Guide)* in first 2 sts, [sc dec in next 2 dc] around, ending with sc in last st. Fasten off. *(10 sc)*

EDGING

Join pink in first st, ch 1, [sl st in next st, ch 1] around, join in beg sl st. Fasten off.

Rep Sleeve and Edging in rem armhole.

Sew snap to top edge of back opening.

FLOWER
MAKE 2.
With pink, ch 4, sl st in 4th ch from hook, [ch 3, sc in same ch] 5 times. Leaving long end, fasten off.

Sew 1 Flower to Bodice as shown in photo. Sew 1 bead to center of Flower. Set rem Flower aside for Hat.

PANTIES
FRONT
Row 1: With white, ch 4, sc in 2nd ch from hook and in each ch across, turn. *(3 sc)*

Row 2 (RS): Ch 1, sc in each st across, turn.

Rows 3–10: Ch 1, 2 sc in first st sc in each st across with 2 sc in last st, turn. At end of last row, fasten off. *(19 sc at end of last row)*

BACK
Row 1: With WS facing, working in starting ch on opposite side of row 1 on Front, join white with sc in first ch, sc in each of next 2 chs, turn. *(3 sc)*

Row 2 (RS): Ch 1, sc in each st across, turn.

Rows 3–10: Ch 1, 2 sc in first st sc in each st across with 2 sc in last st, turn. *(19 sc at end of last row)*

Rnd 11: Now working in rnds, ch 1, 2 sc in first st, sc in each st across with 2 sc in last st, working in sts across row 10 of Front, sc in each st around, **join** *(see Pattern Notes)* in beg sc. *(40 sc)*

Rnd 12: Ch 1, sc in each st around, join in beg sc. Fasten off.

BOOTIE
MAKE 2.
Rnd 1: With white, ch 6, 2 sc in 2nd ch from hook, sc in each of next 2 chs, hdc in next ch, 4 hdc in last ch, working on opposite side of ch, hdc in next ch, sc in each of next 2 chs, 2 sc in last ch, **join** *(see Pattern Notes)* in beg sc. *(14 sts)*

Rnd 2: Ch 1, 2 sc in first st, sc in each of next 3 sts, hdc in next st, 2 hdc in each of next 4 sts, hdc in next st, sc in each of next 3 sts, 2 sc in last st, join in beg sc. *(20 sts)*

Rnd 3: Working in **back lps** *(see Stitch Guide)*, ch 1, sc in each st around, join in beg sc.

Rnd 4: Working in both lps, ch 1, sc in each of first 7 sts, [**sc dec** *(see Stitch Guide)* in next 2 sts] 3 times *(toe)*, sc in each of last 7 sts, join in beg sc. *(17 sc)*

Rnd 5: Ch 1, sc in each of first 7 sts, sc dec in next 3 sts, sc in each of last 7 sts, join in beg sc. *(15 sc)*

Rnd 6: Ch 1, sc in each st around, join in beg sc. Fasten off.

TRIM
Join pink with sc in first st, sc in each st around, join in beg sc. Fasten off.

HAT
Rnd 1: With white, ch 4, 9 dc in 4th ch from hook *(first 3 chs count as first dc)*, **join** *(see Pattern Notes)* in 4th ch of beg ch-4. *(10 dc)*

Rnd 2: Ch 3 *(see Pattern Notes)*,, dc in same st, 2 dc in each st around, join in 3rd ch of beg ch-3. *(20 dc)*

Rnd 3: Rep rnd 2. *(40 dc)*

Rnd 4: Ch 3, dc in same st, dc in next st, [2 dc in next st, dc in next st] around, join in 3rd ch of beg ch-3. *(60 dc)*

Rnd 5: Ch 3, dc in each st around, join in 3rd ch of beg ch-3.

Rnd 6: Ch 2 *(see Pattern Notes)*, dc in next st, [**dc dec** *(see Stitch Guide)* in next 2 sts] around, join in beg dc. *(30 dc)*

Rnd 7: Ch 1, sc in each st around, join in beg sc.

Rnd 8: Working in **back lps** *(see Stitch Guide)*, ch 3, dc in same st, 3 dc in next st, [2 dc in next st, 3 dc in next st] around, join in 3rd ch of beg ch-3. Fasten off. *(75 dc)*

EDGING
Working in rem lps of rnd 7, join in any st, ch 1, [sl st in next st, ch 1] around, join in beg sl st. Fasten off.

Sew rem rose to Hat as shown in photo. Sew rem bead to center of Flower.

BLANKET
SKILL LEVEL

INTERMEDIATE

FINISHED SIZE
5½ inches square

MATERIALS
- Super fine (fingering) weight yarn: 1 oz/175 yds/28g each white and pink
- Size B/1/2.25mm crochet hook or size needed to obtain gauge
- Tapestry needle

1 SUPER FINE

GAUGE
7 sc = 1 inch; 8 sc rows = 1 inch

PATTERN NOTES
Join with slip stitch as indicated unless otherwise stated.

INSTRUCTIONS
BLANKET
SQUARE
MAKE 8 EACH WHITE & PINK.
Row 1 (RS): Ch 9, sc in 2nd ch from hook and in each ch across, turn.

Rows 2–8: Ch 1, sc in each st across, turn.

Rnd 9: Working around outer edge, ch 1, sc in each of first 7 sts, 3 sc in last st, working in ends of rows, sc in each row across, working in starting ch on opposite side of row 1, 3 sc in first ch, sc in each ch across with 3 sc in last ch, sc in end of each row across, 2 sc in same st as beg sc, **join** (see Pattern Note) in beg sc. Fasten off.

EDGING
Using pink on white Squares and white on pink Squares, with RS facing, working in **front lps** (see Stitch Guide), join in any st on rnd 9, ch 2, [sl st in next st, ch 2] around, join in beg sl st. Fasten off.

ASSEMBLY
Working in rem lps of rnd 9, sew Squares tog in 4 rows with 4 Squares in each row, alternating colors as shown in photo. ■

Sleepy Time
PJ's

PJ'S & HAT
SKILL LEVEL

INTERMEDIATE

FINISHED SIZE
Fits 5-inch baby doll

MATERIALS
- Super fine (fingering) weight yarn:
  1 oz/175 yds/28g each blue
  and white
- Size B/1/2.25mm crochet hook
  or size needed to obtain gauge
- Tapestry needle
- Sewing needle
- White sewing thread
- Snap
- Small white pompom
- Stitch markers

1 SUPER FINE

GAUGE
7 sc = 1 inch; 8 sc rows = 1 inch

PATTERN NOTES
Join with slip stitch as indicated unless
  otherwise stated.

Chain-3 at beginning of row or round counts as
  first double crochet unless otherwise stated.

Chain-2 at beginning of row or round **does not**
  count as first stitch unless otherwise stated.

You may make any combination of Circles and
  sew to front of PJ's.

Another option is to leave off Circles and sew
  small buttons or decals on front.

Do not apply small beads or buttons to doll
  clothing that is intended for play by children
  ages 3 or less.

INSTRUCTIONS
PJ'S
FIRST LEG

Rnd 1: Beg at foot, with blue, ch 6, 2 sc in 2nd ch from hook, sc in each of next 2 chs, hdc in next ch, 4 hdc in last ch, working on opposite side of ch, hdc in next ch, sc in next 2 chs, 2 sc in last ch, **join** (*see Pattern Notes*) in beg sc. (*14 sts*)

Rnd 2: Ch 1, 2 sc in first st, sc in each of next 3 sts, hdc in next st, 2 hdc in each of next 4 sts, hdc in next st, sc in each of next 3 sts, 2 sc in last st, join in beg sc. (*20 sts*)

Rnd 3: Ch 1, sc in each st around, join in beg sc.

Rnd 4: Ch 1, sc in each of first 7 sts, [**sc dec** (*see Stitch Guide*) in next 2 sts] 3 times, sc in each of last 7 sts, join in beg sc. (*17 sc*)

Rnd 5: Ch 1, sc in each of first 7 sts, sc dec in next 3 sts, sc in each of last 7 sts, join in beg sc. (*15 sc*)

Rnds 6 & 7: Ch 1, sc in each st around, join in beg sc.

Rnd 8: Ch 3 (*see Pattern Notes*), dc in same st, [dc in next st, 2 dc in next st] around, join in 3rd ch of beg ch-3. (*23 dc*)

Rnd 9: Ch 3, dc in each st around, join in 3rd ch of beg ch-3.

Rnd 10: Ch 3, dc in each of next 18 sts, mark last dc for joining the Legs, dc in each st around, join in 3rd ch of beg ch-3. Fasten off.

2ND LEG
Rnds 1–9: Rep rnds 1–9 of First Leg.

Rnd 10: Ch 3, dc in each st around, join in 3rd ch of beg ch-3.

BODY
Rnd 11: Ch 3, dc in each of next 5 sts, dc in marked st on First Leg, keeping RS facing, dc in each of next 22 sts on First Leg, dc in marked dc again, sl st between 6th dc from 2nd Leg and first dc from First Leg, dc in same dc as 6th dc from 2nd Leg, dc in each rem 17 dc around 2nd Leg, join in 3rd ch of beg ch-3. (*1 sl st, 46 dc*)

Rnd 12: Ch 3, dc in each st around to sl st, **dc dec** (*see Stitch Guide*) in sl st and next st, dc in each st around, join in 3rd ch of beg ch-3.

Rnd 13: Loosely sl st in each of first 6 sts, ch 3, dc in each st around, dc in each of first 6 sl sts, join in 3rd ch of beg ch-3.

Rnd 14: Ch 3, dc in each of next 3 sts, dc dec in next 2 sts, [dc in each of next 4 sts, dc dec in next 2 sts] 6 times, dc in each of last 5 sts, join in 3rd ch of beg ch-3. (*40 dc*)

Row 15: Now working in rows, ch 3, dc each st around, turn, **do not join**.

Row 16: Ch 3, dc in each st across, turn.

Row 17: Ch 3, dc in each of next 9 sts, ch 8, sk next 4 sts (*armhole*), dc in each of next 12 sts, ch 8, sk next 4 sts (*armhole*), dc in each of last 10 sts, turn. (*16 chs, 32 dc*)

Row 18: Ch 3, dc in each of first 10 sts, sc in each of next 8 chs, dc in each of next 12 sts, sc in each of next 8 chs, dc in each of last 10 sts, turn. (*16 sc, 32 dc*)

Row 19: Ch 1, sc dec in first 2 sts, [sc dec in next 2 sts] across, turn. (*24 sc*)

Row 20: Ch 1, sc in each st across. Fasten off.

SLEEVE
Rnd 1: Join blue in first sk st on row 16, ch 3, dc in each of next 3 sts, 4 dc in end of next row, dc in each of next 8 chs, 4 dc in end of next row, join in 3rd ch of beg ch-3. (*20 dc*)

Rnds 2 & 3: Ch 3, dc in each st around, join in 3rd ch of beg ch-3.

Rnd 4: Ch 1, sc dec in first 2 sts, [sc dec in next 2 sts] around, join in beg sc. (*10 sc*)

Rnd 5: Ch 1, sc in each st around, join in beg sc. Fasten off.

Rep Sleeve in rem armhole.

Sew snap to top edge of back opening.

LARGE CIRCLE

Rnd 1: With white, **ch 2** *(see Pattern Notes)*, 6 sc in 2nd ch from hook, join in beg sc. *(6 sc)*

Rnd 2: Ch 1, 2 sc in first st and in each st around, join in beg sc. *(12 sc)*

Rnd 3: Ch 1, sc in first st, 2 sc in next st, [sc in next st, 2 sc in next st] around, join in beg sc. *(18 sc)*

Rnd 4: Ch 1, sc in each of first 2 sts, 2 sc in next st, [sc in each of first 2 sts, 2 sc in next st] around, join in beg sc. Leaving long end, fasten off. *(24 sc)*

MEDIUM CIRCLE

Rnds 1–3: Rep rnds 1–3 of Large Circle. At end of last rnd, leaving long end, fasten off. *(18 sc)*

SMALL CIRCLE

Rnds 1 & 2: Rep rnds 1 and 2 of Large Circle. At end of last rnd, leaving long end, fasten off. *(12 sc)*

TINY CIRCLE

With white, ch 2, 6 sc in 2nd ch from hook, join in beg sc. Fasten off. *(6 sc)*

Sew Circles *(see Pattern Notes)* to front of PJ's as shown in photo.

HAT

Rnd 1: With blue, ch 36, sl st in first ch to form ring, being careful not to twist ch, ch 1, sc in each ch around, **join** *(see Pattern Notes)* in beg sc. *(36 sc)*

Rnd 2: Ch 1, sc in each st around, join in beg sc.

Rnd 3: Ch 1, sc in each st around, join in beg sc. Fasten off.

Rnd 4: Join white with sc in first st, sc in each st around, join in beg sc.

Rnd 5: Ch 1, sc in each st around, join in beg sc.

Rnd 6: Ch 1, sc in each st around, join in beg sc. Fasten off.

Rnd 7: Join blue with sc in first st, sc in each st around, join in beg sc.

Rnd 8: Ch 1, sc in each st around, join in beg sc.

Rnd 9: Ch 1, sc in each of first 4 sts, **sc dec** *(see Stitch Guide)* in next 2 sts, [sc in each of next 4 sts, sc dec in next 2 sts] around, join in beg sc. Fasten off. *(30 sc)*

Rnd 10: Join white with sc in first st, sc in each st around, join in beg sc.

Rnd 11: Ch 1, sc in each st around, join in beg sc.

Rnd 12: Ch 1, sc in each st around, join in beg sc. Fasten off.

Rnd 13: Join blue with sc in first st, sc in each st around, join in beg sc.

Rnd 14: Ch 1, sc in each st around, join in beg sc.

Rnd 15: Ch 1, sc in each of first 3 sts, sc dec in next 2 sts, [sc in each of next 3 sts, sc dec in next 2 sts] around, join in beg sc. Fasten off. *(24 sc)*

Rnd 16: Join white with sc in first st, sc in each st around, join in beg sc.

Rnds 17 & 18: Rep rnds 11 and 12.

Rnd 19: Join blue with sc in first st, sc in each st around, join in beg sc.

Rnd 20: Ch 1, sc in each st around, join in beg sc.

Rnd 21: Ch 1, sc in each of first 2 sts, sc dec in next 2 sts, [sc in each of next 2 sts, sc dec in next 2 sts] around, join in beg sc. Fasten off. *(18 sc)*

Rnd 22: Join white with sc in first st, sc in each st around, join in beg sc.

Rnds 23 & 24: Rep rnds 11 and 12.

Rnd 25: Join blue with sc in first st, sc in each st around, join in beg sc.

Rnd 26: Ch 1, sc in each st around, join in beg sc.

Rnd 27: Ch 1, sc in first st, sc dec in next 2 sts, [sc in next st, sc dec in next 2 sts] around, join in beg sc. Fasten off. *(12 sc)*

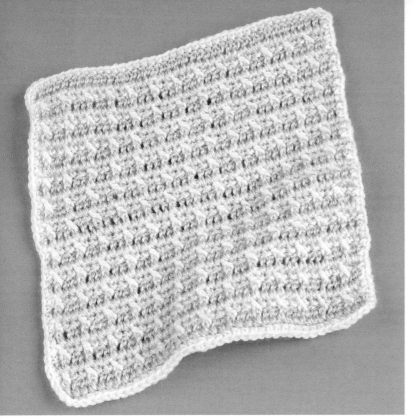

Rnd 28: Join white with sc in first st, sc in each st around, join in beg sc.

Rnds 29 & 30: Rep rnds 11 and 12.

Rnd 31: Join blue with sc in first st, sc in each st around, join in beg sc.

Rnd 32: Ch 1, sc in each st around, join in beg sc.

Rnd 33: Ch 1, sc dec in first 2 sts, [sc dec in next 2 sts] around, join in beg sc. Leaving long end, fasten off. *(6 sc)*

Weave long end through top of sts on rnd 33, pull to close. Secure end.

Sew pompom to point of Hat.

Fold rnd 33 down and tack to side of Hat.

BLANKET

SKILL LEVEL

INTERMEDIATE

FINISHED SIZE
5½ inches square

MATERIALS
■ Super fine (fingering) weight yarn: 1 oz/175 yds/28g each blue and white

SUPER FINE

■ Size B/1/2.25mm crochet hook or size needed to obtain gauge
■ Tapestry needle

GAUGE
7 sc = 1 inch; 4 pattern rows = 1 inch

PATTERN NOTES
Join with slip stitch as indicated unless otherwise stated.

When working this pattern, you can either fasten off each color when changing colors or work over the color that is now being used.

Always **change colors** *(see Stitch Guide)* in last stitch worked.

Chain-3 at beginning of row or round counts as first double crochet unless otherwise stated.

INSTRUCTIONS
BLANKET
Row 1: With blue, ch 42, dc in 4th ch from hook *(first 3 chs count as first dc)* and in each ch across, **changing colors** *(see Pattern Notes)* to white, turn. *(40 dc)*

Row 2: Ch 1, sc in each of first 2 sts, **fphdc** *(see Stitch Guide)* around next st, [sc in each of next 2 sts, fphdc around next st] across, ending with sc in last st, changing to blue, turn.

Row 3: Ch 3 *(see Pattern Notes)*, dc in each st across, changing to white, turn.

Rows 4–25: [Rep rows 2 and 3 alternately for pattern] 11 times.

At end of last row, fasten off blue.

EDGING
Working around outer edge, ch 1, sc in each st across with 3 sc in last st, working in ends of rows, evenly sp sc across, working in starting ch on opposite side of row 1, 3 sc in first ch, sc in each ch across with 3 sc in last ch, working in ends of rows, evenly sp sc across, 2 sc in same st as beg sc, **join** *(see Pattern Notes)* in beg sc. Fasten off. ■

All-Star
Romper

SKILL LEVEL

INTERMEDIATE

FINISHED SIZE
Fits 5-inch baby doll

MATERIALS
- Super fine (fingering) weight yarn:
  1 oz/175 yds/28g each blue
  and white
- Size B/1/2.25mm crochet hook
  or size needed to obtain gauge
- Tapestry needle
- Sewing needle
- Matching sewing thread
- Snaps: 2
- Small, star-shaped buttons: 2

1 SUPER FINE

GAUGE
7 sc = 1 inch; 8 sc rows = 1 inch

PATTERN NOTES
Join with slip stitch as indicated unless
  otherwise stated.

Chain-3 at beginning of row or round counts as
  first double crochet unless otherwise stated.

Do not apply small beads or buttons to doll
  clothing that is intended for play by children
  ages 3 or less.

INSTRUCTIONS
ROMPER
Row 1: Beg at neck, with blue, ch 25, 2 sc in 2nd
  ch from hook and in each ch across, turn. *(48 sc)*

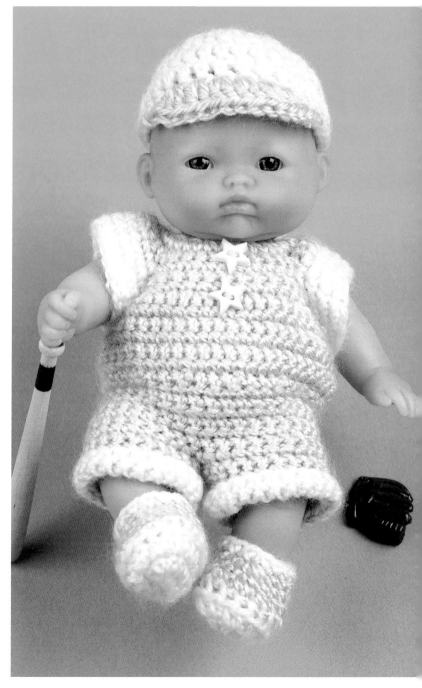

Row 2: Ch 1, sc in each st across, turn.

Row 3 (RS): Ch 1, sc in each of first 8 sts, ch 5, sk next 10 sts *(armhole)*, sc in each of next 12 sts, ch 5, sk next 10 sts *(armhole)*, sc in each of last 8 sts, turn. *(10 chs, 28 sc)*

Row 4: Ch 1, sc in each st and in each ch across, turn. *(38 sc)*

Row 5: Ch 1, sc in each st across, turn.

Row 6: Ch 1, sc in each of first 2 sts, [2 sc in next st, sc in each of next 2 sts] across, turn. *(50 sc)*

Rows 7–10: Ch 1, sc in each st across, turn.

Rnd 11: Now working in rnds, ch 1, sc in each st around, **join** *(see Pattern Notes)* in beg sc.

Rnd 12: Ch 1, sc in each of first 2 sts, [**sc dec** *(see Stitch Guide)* in next 2 sts, sc in each of next 2 sts] around, join in beg sc. *(38 sc)*

Rnds 13–18: Ch 1, sc in each st around, join in beg sc.

FIRST LEG
Rnd 1: Ch 3, sk next 18 sts, sc in next st, ch 1, sc in same st and in each st around, sc in each of first 3 chs, join in beg sc. *(22 sc)*

Rnds 2–4: Ch 1, sc in each st around, join in beg sc. At end of last rnd, fasten off.

CUFF
Rnd 1: With RS facing and neckline pointed down, working in **front lps** *(see Stitch Guide)*, join white with sc in first st, sc in each st around, join in beg sc.

Rnd 2: Ch 1, sc in each st around, join in beg sc. Fasten off.

Fold Cuff up.

2ND LEG
Rnd 1: Join blue with sc in joining sc on rnd 18 of Romper, sc in each of next 18 sts, sc in each of next 3 chs, join in beg sc. *(22 sc)*

Rnds 2–4: Ch 1, sc in each st around, join in beg sc. At end of last rnd, fasten off.

CUFF
Rep Cuff of First Leg.

SLEEVE
Rnd 1: Join white with sc in center ch of ch-5 on armhole, sc in each of next 2 chs, 2 sc in end of next row, sc in each of next 10 sts, 2 sc in end of next row, sc in each of last 2 chs, join in beg sc. *(19 sc)*

Rnds 2–4: Ch 1, sc in each st around, join in beg sc. At end of rnd 4, fasten off.

Rep Sleeve in rem armhole.

Sew snaps to back opening.

Sew buttons on front as shown in photo.

BOOTIE
MAKE 2.
Rnd 1: With white, ch 6, 2 sc in 2nd ch from hook, sc in each of next 2 chs, hdc in next ch, 4 hdc in last ch, working on opposite side of ch, hdc in next ch, sc in each of next 2 chs, 2 sc in last ch, join in beg sc. *(14 sts)*

Rnd 2: Ch 1, 2 sc in first st, sc in each of next 3 sts, hdc in next st, 2 hdc in each of next 4 sts *(toe)*, hdc in next st, sc in each of next 3 sts, 2 sc in last st, join in beg sc. Fasten off. *(20 sts)*

Rnd 3: Working in **back lps** *(see Stitch Guide)*, join blue with sc in first st, sc in each st around, join in beg sc.

Rnd 4: Ch 1, sc in each of first 7 sts, [sc dec in next 2 sts] 3 times, sc in each of last 7 sts, join in beg sc. *(17 sc)*

Rnd 5: Ch 1, sc in each of first 7 sts, sc dec in next 3 sts, sc in each of last 7 sts, join in beg sc.

Rnd 6: Ch 1, sc in each st around, join in beg sc. Fasten off.

Rnd 7: Join white with sc in first st, sc in each st around, join in beg sc. Fasten off.

HAT

Rnd 1: With white, ch 4, 9 dc in 4th ch from hook *(first 3 chs count as first dc)*, **join** *(see Pattern Notes)* in 4th ch of beg ch-4. *(10 dc)*

Rnd 2: **Ch 3** *(see Pattern Notes)*, dc in same st, 2 dc in each st around, join in 3rd ch of beg ch-3. *(20 dc)*

Rnd 3: Ch 3, dc in same st, dc in next st, [2 dc in next st, dc in next st] around, join in 3rd ch of beg ch-3. *(30 dc)*

Rnds 4 & 5: Ch 3, dc in each st around, join in 3rd ch of beg ch-3. At end of last rnd, fasten off.

BILL

Join blue in first st, sc in next st, hdc in next st, 2 dc in each of next 6 sts, hdc in next st, sc in next st, sl st in next st, leaving rem sts unworked. Fasten off. ∎

STITCH GUIDE

STITCH ABBREVIATIONS

beg	begin/begins/beginning
bpdc	back post double crochet
bpsc	back post single crochet
bptr	back post treble crochet
CC	contrasting color
ch(s)	chain(s)
ch-	refers to chain or space previously made (i.e., ch-1 space)
ch sp(s)	chain space(s)
cl(s)	cluster(s)
cm	centimeter(s)
dc	double crochet (singular/plural)
dc dec	double crochet 2 or more stitches together, as indicated
dec	decrease/decreases/decreasing
dtr	double treble crochet
ext	extended
fpdc	front post double crochet
fpsc	front post single crochet
fptr	front post treble crochet
g	gram(s)
hdc	half double crochet
hdc dec	half double crochet 2 or more stitches together, as indicated
inc	increase/increases/increasing
lp(s)	loop(s)
MC	main color
mm	millimeter(s)
oz	ounce(s)
pc	popcorn(s)
rem	remain/remains/remaining
rep(s)	repeat(s)
rnd(s)	round(s)
RS	right side
sc	single crochet (singular/plural)
sc dec	single crochet 2 or more stitches together, as indicated
sk	skip/skipped/skipping
sl st(s)	slip stitch(es)
sp(s)	space(s)/spaced
st(s)	stitch(es)
tog	together
tr	treble crochet
trtr	triple treble
WS	wrong side
yd(s)	yard(s)
yo	yarn over

YARN CONVERSION

OUNCES TO GRAMS		GRAMS TO OUNCES	
1	28.4	25	7/8
2	56.7	40	1 2/3
3	85.0	50	1 3/4
4	113.4	100	3 1/2

UNITED STATES		UNITED KINGDOM
sl st (slip stitch)	=	sc (single crochet)
sc (single crochet)	=	dc (double crochet)
hdc (half double crochet)	=	htr (half treble crochet)
dc (double crochet)	=	tr (treble crochet)
tr (treble crochet)	=	dtr (double treble crochet)
dtr (double treble crochet)	=	ttr (triple treble crochet)
skip	=	miss

Single crochet decrease (sc dec): (Insert hook, yo, draw lp through) in each of the sts indicated, yo, draw through all lps on hook.

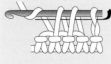

Example of 2-sc dec

Half double crochet decrease (hdc dec): (Yo, insert hook, yo, draw lp through) in each of the sts indicated, yo, draw through all lps on hook.

Example of 2-hdc dec

Reverse single crochet (reverse sc): Ch 1, sk first st, working from left to right, insert hook in next st from front to back, draw up lp on hook, yo, and draw through both lps on hook.

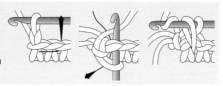

Chain (ch): Yo, pull through lp on hook.

Single crochet (sc): Insert hook in st, yo, pull through st, yo, pull through both lps on hook.

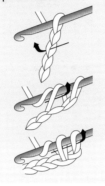

Double crochet (dc): Yo, insert hook in st, yo, pull through st, [yo, pull through 2 lps] twice.

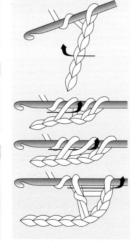

Double crochet decrease (dc dec): (Yo, insert hook, yo, draw lp through, yo, draw through 2 lps on hook) in each of the sts indicated, yo, draw through all lps on hook.

Example of 2-dc dec

Front loop (front lp) Back loop (back lp)

Front Loop   Back Loop

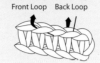

Front post stitch (fp): Back post stitch (bp): When working post st, insert hook from right to left around post of st on previous row.

Back   Front

Post of Stitch

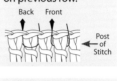

Half double crochet (hdc): Yo, insert hook in st, yo, pull through st, yo, pull through all 3 lps on hook.

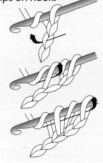

Double treble crochet (dtr): Yo 3 times, insert hook in st, yo, pull through st, [yo, pull through 2 lps] 4 times.

Treble crochet decrease (tr dec): Holding back last lp of each st, tr in each of the sts indicated, yo, pull through all lps on hook.

Example of 2-tr dec

Slip stitch (sl st): Insert hook in st, pull through both lps on hook.

Chain color change (ch color change) Yo with new color, draw through last lp on hook.

Double crochet color change (dc color change) Drop first color, yo with new color, draw through last 2 lps of st.

Treble crochet (tr): Yo twice, insert hook in st, yo, pull through st, [yo, pull through 2 lps] 3 times.

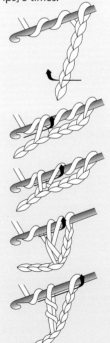

Metric Conversion Charts

METRIC CONVERSIONS

yards	x	.9144	=	metres (m)
yards	x	91.44	=	centimetres (cm)
inches	x	2.54	=	centimetres (cm)
inches	x	25.40	=	millimetres (mm)
inches	x	.0254	=	metres (m)

centimetres	x	.3937	=	inches
metres	x	1.0936	=	yards

INCHES INTO MILLIMETRES & CENTIMETRES (Rounded off slightly)

inches	mm	cm	inches	cm	inches	cm	inches	cm
1/8	3	0.3	5	12.5	21	53.5	38	96.5
1/4	6	0.6	5 1/2	14	22	56	39	99
3/8	10	1	6	15	23	58.5	40	101.5
1/2	13	1.3	7	18	24	61	41	104
5/8	15	1.5	8	20.5	25	63.5	42	106.5
3/4	20	2	9	23	26	66	43	109
7/8	22	2.2	10	25.5	27	68.5	44	112
1	25	2.5	11	28	28	71	45	114.5
1 1/4	32	3.2	12	30.5	29	73.5	46	117
1 1/2	38	3.8	13	33	30	76	47	119.5
1 3/4	45	4.5	14	35.5	31	79	48	122
2	50	5	15	38	32	81.5	49	124.5
2 1/2	65	6.5	16	40.5	33	84	50	127
3	75	7.5	17	43	34	86.5		
3 1/2	90	9	18	46	35	89		
4	100	10	19	48.5	36	91.5		
4 1/2	115	11.5	20	51	37	94		

KNITTING NEEDLES CONVERSION CHART

Canada/U.S.	0	1	2	3	4	5	6	7	8	9	10	10½	11	13	15
Metric (mm)	2	2¼	2¾	3¼	3½	3¾	4	4½	5	5½	6	6½	8	9	10

CROCHET HOOKS CONVERSION CHART

Canada/U.S.	1/B	2/C	3/D	4/E	5/F	6/G	8/H	9/I	10/J	10½/K	N
Metric (mm)	2.25	2.75	3.25	3.5	3.75	4.25	5	5.5	6	6.5	9.0

Itty Bitty Dress-Up Fashions is published by DRG, 306 East Parr Road, Berne, IN 46711. Printed in USA. Copyright © 2011 DRG.

RETAIL STORES: If you would like to carry this pattern book or any other DRG publications, visit DRGwholesale.com.

Every effort has been made to ensure that the instructions in this publication are complete and accurate.
We cannot, however, take responsibility for human error, typographical mistakes or variations in individual work.
Please visit AnniesCustomerCare.com to check for pattern updates.

ISBN: 978-1-59635-367-1

3 4 5 6 7 8 9